NO MORE HIRING REGRETS

by Kristin Heller

The information in this book is intended for educational and informational purposes only.

No More Hiring Regrets

Copyright © 2023 by Kristin Heller

All rights reserved. No part of this book may be reproduced or used in any manner without written permission of the copyright owner except for the use of quotations in a book review. For more information, address: Kristin@HRCreativeconsulting.com.

First edition 2023

www.HRCreativeConsulting.com

A Note from the Author

I'm Kristin Heller, and I have been practicing human resources, talent management, coaching and development for over 25 years. One thing I have learned over the years is that most business leaders, from front-line supervisors to executive level positions, do not know how to conduct an effective interview. I have seen it over and over.

Business leaders that understand what it means to truly interview a candidate have a better shot at making a solid, effective hire. How to conduct an interview is not taught in leadership training and yet interviewing and building strong teams is one of the most important tasks for business leaders.

I have worked with dozens of leaders over the years. A small percentage of them understand the importance and impact of a meaningful interview. What is scarier is that only once, in my entire career, did someone ask me how to conduct an interview (shout out to Luke).

This book is intended to guide small businesses and new leaders in their interview process to make better hires. Make great hires to build strong businesses.

This is for my Dad.
Thank you for being one of the good ones.

To Clint, Bob and Brian...Thank you.

Contents

Chapter One: Did Anyone Teach You How to Conduct an Interview?

Chapter Two: Commit the Time. Never Settle – Round One

Chapter Three: Understand Your Business Needs

Chapter Four: The Candidate Search

Chapter Five: Commit the Time. Never Settle – Round Two

Chapter Six: FINALLY! Time to Start Interviewing

Chapter Seven: Candidate Questions

Chapter Eight: Beware of Interview Bias

Chapter Nine: You Are in This Too!

Chapter Ten: Commit the Time. Never Settle – Final Round

Chapter Eleven: Make the Offer

Chapter Twelve: Just a Few More Things...

Chapter Thirteen: Wrap-Up

Additional Resources

Interview Deck

The information in this book is for general informational and educational purposes only. I am not an employment attorney nor am I providing legal advice. Information in this book is based solely on my experiences. It is advised that you consult an attorney with any questions or concerns regarding employment, employment law or your hiring process. If it doesn't feel right, don't do it. Call a lawyer.

I have made every effort to ensure the accuracy of the information within this book was correct at the time of publication. I do not assume and hereby disclaim any liability to any party for any loss, damage, or disruption caused by errors or omissions, whether such errors or omissions result from accident, negligence, or any other cause.

Please note that I don't make any guarantees about the results of the information in this book. I share my many recruiting experiences that are intended to help you succeed in your recruiting process. You, nevertheless, need to know that your ultimate success or failure will be the result of your own efforts, your particular situation, and innumerable other circumstances beyond my knowledge and control.

CHAPTER ONE

Did Anyone Teach You How to Conduct an Interview?

I'm here to show you how to interview candidates.

Have you ever been coached on how to conduct an interview? There is some unease around interviewing, and there should be some unease if you have never done it before. It is a process to be developed, over time with practice. That said, interviewing and hiring are part of doing business. So, why don't we focus more on interviewing? Why don't we conduct training on interviewing?

The feeling of unease lies around the unknown. Are you afraid of making a poor hiring decision? Do you know what to ask your candidates? Are you uncomfortable because you don't know enough about interviewing? Do you know what you are going to pay your new hire? I will answer these questions so you can interview your candidates, build great teams and continue to grow your business.

I am not here to tell you whether or not your business needs an employee, but I can provide you with some tools to help you prepare for adding your new hire. I will provide you with tips, templates, and some of my experiences to help you interview and hire the best person for your organization.

No one, and I mean no one is a perfect interviewer. Even the most skilled interviewers get it wrong from time to time. When you are interviewing, you are doing your best to assess your candidates and there is no exact science to reading people. With some practice, you get better at interviewing. You develop skills that help you identify what may or may not work in your business but in the end, no one gets it right every single time.

Yes. There are some things you need to know about conducting interviews. This book will guide you through the key elements. Focus on the following tips and tools. As you gain experience with candidates, you will strengthen your interviewing skills.

HR professionals interview candidates -- many candidates. In my first HR role, I was told to hire. So I set out to do just that. Hire some people. I had no clue how to conduct an interview.

Back then, resources were far more limited, so I did what every trying-to-make-an-impression-new-HR-manager would do: I put on my HR game face and I faked it. I was going to do my best, and I was going to wing it! Despite my lack of experience and through many mishaps, I figured it out and I began to hire. It is my goal to save you time, offer some tips, tools and share what I learned over the years.

The experience of winging it taught me that I needed and wanted a process. I needed to create a plan for recruiting and hiring. After all, this was going to be part of my career. I began to organize, create questions, and most importantly, I began to understand the roles and needs of our business.

When it comes to hiring, there is a process to getting a new person into an open role. The size of your organization will play a role in what steps you may be able to skip, but there are some steps you should never skip. Bypassing the steps in this process may lead to poor candidate pools or worse, a poor hiring choice. I hope to help you reduce your risk of making a poor hiring decision.

Let's face it. We are all human. There is no way to guarantee you are going to nail it when you make your hiring decision, but there are steps you can take to help you clear out those candidates that are not a good fit for you, your business and your open position. When hiring, you are looking for the best technical and organizational fit for your business.

As you are interviewing, you will hit it off with some candidates more than others. It is always great to make a connection, but make sure they can do the job. Hitting it off and being successful in the role are not the same thing. Can they contribute? Can they be successful in the role? Equally as important, do they fit in? It is fine to have the brightest, most qualified candidate for your organization but if they are challenging, combative or they cannot effectively communicate, are they the best hire for your role? The ideal candidate for any role, for any organization, is both – an organizational and technical fit* – providing them the best opportunity to succeed in the role.

Throughout the book, I use the words technical or technical fit. I am referring to a candidate's skills that are specific to their role.

During the entire interviewing and hiring process, it is important to never lose sight of your business goal: **Hire the person that is the best overall fit for your organization.** I will remind you of this goal throughout the book.

To get started, let's map out your process using the tools and guidelines in this book.

CHAPTER TWO

Commit the Time
Never Settle
Round One

This is really important.

Throughout this book, I will harp on two important topics - commit the time and never settle. With regards to the sourcing, interviewing and the hiring process, your commitment to the process and the time it takes out of your day may become frustrating, but it will pay off in the long run. Your commitment to never settle will pay off even bigger in the long run.

I will continue to talk about the importance of committing your time to this process. You feel you don't have the time. I get it. Make the time. Block time on your calendar and leave it blocked. By committing the time and committing to the process, you will reduce your risk of dealing with a poor hiring decision. There is no guarantee when hiring; but I can tell you from personal experience, if you rush the process and settle on a less-than-desirable candidate, you increase your odds of a poor choice and potential problems down the road.

Rushing through interviews will cause you to miss something. You will skip questions or worse, avoid the questions all together and simply spark up a conversation. A conversation is not an interview, and it will not give you insight into your candidate. Do not rush the process.

If you allow your busy schedule to get in the way of the interview process, you will settle on a candidate. There is a good chance you will have to start over. Hiring is an investment in your business. Why would you want anyone less than ideal on your team? The candidate you select should be the best candidate for your role. They should not simply be good enough. Never give in to "good enough".

Commit the time. Never settle.

CHAPTER THREE

Understand Your Business Needs

How to know what to look for in your candidates.

If a current employee resigns, it is slightly less complicated to replace them if you understand the role the employee filled. If that is the case, you can skip over the next section.

If you are adding a new position, there are more things to consider. It is important to understand the current state of your organization.

Your entire organization whether it is a large or small group of employees:
- Is feeling stretched thin
- Working long hours with few breaks
- They are telling you they need help
- They are telling you they need a break

My first bit of advice is to Listen! Always listen to your team and always listen to yourself. They are speaking up because they need to be heard.

My next piece of advice is to understand what they are really saying:
- They are asking for help.
- Consider the strain on your business.
- Is it cost-effective to hire?
- Will a new hire ease the burden on your business?
- Will a new hire ease the burden on your team?
- Can your business support additional headcount?
- Is a new hire going to solve the problem?

After careful consideration and a significant amount of listening to the same complaint over and over you decide the cost of a new hire outweighs the cost to wait and you determine it is time to add some help. Great! Now what?

It is critical to understand exactly what your business needs and exactly how your new hire will fill those gaps.

Are your technical experts spending time doing administrative tasks? If so, perhaps you need a support person. Are your technical experts so overwhelmed with technical work that they simply need more technical help? If so, hire another technical person.

Weigh the value of the needs. What is a new hire going to do to make the business run more smoothly or to reduce the strain on your business, your team and you? This is the question you must be able to answer before you can figure out what type of role you need to fill.

Once you determine the role, create a job description. Don't panic. A job description does not need to be anything formal. There is no need to spend time creating a complicated job description.

That said, there *are* things you need to know before you begin your talent search. Review and complete the items listed below to prepare you for your search.

1. Create a task list of all of the things you would like this new hire to do each day.
2. What are the *essential functions* of this role? The essential functions are the tasks the person in the position must be able to

complete. A nonessential function is a task that someone else could complete.
3. Categorize your list by similar tasks and priority of importance. This will help you determine what skill set you require and give you the ability to rank by priority to help you rate your candidates.
4. Will this role be full-time or part-time?
5. Is this a salaried position or hourly? This is your business, but hourly versus salary is determined by the FLSA (Fair Labor Standards Act). For more information, you can reference the following website: www.dol.gov/agencies/whd/compliance-assistance/handy-reference-guide-flsa
6. What is the pay range for this role? This will require some research. The pay should be competitive to the position, your location, your industry, and your company size. The pay range should be determined by the market; not what you want to pay or what your candidates are requesting. Do your homework.
    - Pay transparency is a growing topic. Several states (and some cities) have laws around pay transparency. It is important to know the laws in your state.
    - Many states have laws prohibiting employers from asking a candidate their current salary. It is, however, acceptable to ask a candidate their salary expectations.
    - In addition, many states (and some cities) have a requirement to post position salaries or salary ranges.
7. Is this an in-the-office position? Work from home? Hybrid? Determine this up front so it is not an issue later.
8. To whom will this person report?

9. What, if any, are the educational requirements? If specific education/degree is not needed, do not require it.
10. Are you requiring experience or is this an entry-level position?

A Position Assessment (aka: job description) Template is included in your Interview Deck in the back of the book.

Create a document or complete the included Position Assessment Template to get you focused and organized with your search process. Remember your goal: **Hire the person that is the best overall fit for your organization.** You will be selling your organization to your candidates. Being organized in your hiring process is key.

The job description you have created will serve as the information you need to create your job posting. Be thorough.

I want to make a side note about compensation. Compensation has little to do with interviewing, but it has everything to do with attracting candidates. You want to compensate fairly but you do not want to over-compensate for the position. If you overpay, it can stress your business. It can stifle the growth of the employee. It can cause wage issues if you fill the same or similar roles at a later time. If you underpay, you may not attract or retain candidates and new hires. The trick is to find the sweet spot between what you can pay, what the candidate wants, and what the market deems reasonable.

I recommend erring on the side of caution with compensation.. It is easy to increase pay but almost impossible to reduce or freeze pay and retain the employee. Do your research to create a pay range for the role.

There are dozens of options to assist you with creating pay ranges based on your location, industry, current market, and the position. You can start with The U.S. Bureau of Labor Statistics. Some sources will be high, some will be low. I would recommend comparing a few. Determine an average and create a range. A pay range gives you flexibility.

As you create a salary range, it is important to consider benefits as a part of total compensation. Does your company offer:
- Health care benefits
- Paid time off
- Holiday pay
- Retiree plans ie: 401k plans
- Flexible work hours

All of these elements are part of total compensation. Depending on the size of your company you may or may not offer any employee benefits or perks. If you do not offer any, increase your salary range. These perks are all part of being competitive.

Now that you have clarified the skills needed for your open position and determined a pay range, you are ready to move forward.

CHAPTER FOUR

The Candidate Search

How to find the right people to interview.

Some organizations have the luxury of an applicant tracking system to capture all candidates and applicants. Smaller organizations typically do not, and that is perfectly fine. However, I would suggest using a separate email address for receiving applications. Otherwise, your business email will be full of resumes, CVs, and applications. You will thank me for this later.

It is time to create your job post. The job posting is a candidate's first glimpse into your company. A job posting should be clear on what exactly you want in a candidate. Your post should grab attention without being overwhelming. You do not need to list every single little detail of the job. You do want to list the key activities.

Grab your job description for reference. A job posting should include:
- Job title
- Required skills
- Qualifications
- Location
- Salary and benefits information

Let's break these down.

Job title: Create a job title that means something but is not too vague. For example, if you are hiring an engineer, be specific about the type of engineer ie: electrical, mechanical, civil...you get the point. Using the same example, you do not want to create a job title for a "technical expert". What does that even mean? Do not include numbers in your job title ie: electrical engineer II. Again, what does that mean? Whatever it means to you will have a different meaning at a different organization.

If you want experience, specify the years you require. If it is an entry-level, say that you will train or that you are looking for a recent college graduate.

Required skills: What skill set does a candidate need to be successful in the role? Be specific. For example, qualified candidates must be able to read electrical blueprints. If a position is entry-level, state that you will provide training.

Qualifications: Qualifications consist of accomplishments and experiences the candidate has previously achieved. For example: CPA is required. If a degree or certification is not necessary for success in a role, do not require it. If a role is entry-level, don't ask for a long list of unnecessary qualifications.

Location: Provide a location to rule out candidates that will not travel to you. If you are paying for a relocation, state it in your posting.

Salary and benefits information: Some states are now requiring that salary ranges are included in job postings. Make sure you know what your state requires. Required or not, list the pay range. It is a good filter. It will save you and your candidate time. It will keep the right players in the game. As far as benefits go, it is not necessary to go into details at this point but you can let your candidates know that you do provide medical, dental, etc.

One last note on job postings. Don't make up cute posts using buzzwords. Be professional, factual and specific. Cute is tired and buzzwords are phony.

When you are ready to post your positions, there are several options. Some options are free. Many are at a minimal cost and some are very pricey.

Posting tips:
1. If you are looking for a very specific set of skills, you may want to consider the national organizations of such skills. Oftentimes, professional associations have sites for job postings. If you are a member, you may be able to post your job for free.
2. Sites such as Indeed or LinkedIn are great and widespread. Posting on large, widely used sites will allow for more visibility. Additionally, those sites allow you to share the post with your entire network.
3. Check with your city or county offices. They may offer some job posting options as well.

Employee referrals can be a great source of candidate flow. Offer an incentive to your employees if they recommend candidates and their recommendation gets hired.

This is the part where I put on my HR hat and caution you on employee referrals and the hiring of family members. As the business leader, it is your call on whether or not you allow family and close friends to work in your business. I do not recommend allowing a family member to be in the same department and never, ever should a family member directly report to another family member. Everything is great with family until it isn't. Things do go wrong and when that happens, the family will always win. As far as friend referrals, my only word of caution is the same as with family: everything is great until it isn't. I am jumping off my soapbox now.

Review your applicants
Some positions get many applications, some do not. It is always better to have many options but sifting through many applicants takes time. Commit the time!

Read through all applications. Chances are, you will be able to sort through them quickly for the basics of your business needs. It always worked best for me to create three stacks or folders: Yes, No and Maybe. You can look at your maybes if you run out of yeses.

If you have many applicants, pick a cut-off date. After that date, do not review any additional resumes. If you do not pick a cutoff date, the process will go on and on. You can always go back later and review those candidates if you do not find your ideal candidate in round one.

Give a second look at your yes candidate resumes. Based on your business need, choose 6 to 8 for an initial telephone screen. This may sound like too many candidates to consider, but you likely will not reach all of them or they may have moved on by the time you get to them. I like to have a buffer.

I don't need to tell you, but Covid has changed everything. The hiring process is no exception. I like to conduct an initial telephone screen. It is my personal preference. I keep the telephone screen in my process for the following reasons:

1. Initial ice breaker
2. Understand salary expectations early to save time later
3. Narrow the pool if you have many candidates
4. Clarify anything that may not be clear on their resume
5. Clarify anything that may be of concern to you
6. Makes the first face-to-face interview less stressful and less formal as you have already had a conversation

Telephone screens do not need to be long. They should run no longer than 15 to 20 minutes. Narrow your questions to 3, no more than 4, high-level questions. Save the in-depth interview questions for your face-to-face interview or video interview.

A Telephone Screen Template is included in your Interview Deck in the back of the book.

When talking with your candidates, you will likely determine 1 of 3 things:
1. Move to the next step
2. Maybe
3. Nope, not going to happen

That said, be prepared with a format to end your telephone screen, based on the 3 items above. Here are some easy methods for ending your telephone screen to fit any one of these scenarios:

For your YES candidates, end your call with, *"I would like to move forward and schedule you for an interview."* Sometimes you just know. If you know, schedule it.

For your MAYBE candidates, end your call with, *"I am still in the process of conducting telephone interviews. If you are selected to advance to the next step, I will be in touch by <date> to schedule your interview."* If you are unsure about the candidate, complete all of your telephone screens, then make your decision.

For your NO candidates, end your call with, *"Thank you for your time, however, your skill set does not match our needs for this role. I will keep your resume/cv on file and if anything changes or if something more suited to your skillset opens up, I may reach back out to you. Thank you again for your time and your interest in our organization."* If you know you are not advancing the candidate, don't waste any more of your time or their time.

Commit the time. Start making calls.

CHAPTER FIVE

Commit the Time
Never Settle
Round Two

Is this sinking in yet?

Remember when we talked about committing the time in chapter one? Well, it's back, and I am here to remind you. Sourcing, interviewing, hiring and onboarding is a process. It is a process that takes time. It can be frustrating. It can test your patience. There are times you may need to start over. Yet, you still need to commit the time.

I get it. I have been there. I have wanted to walk away from recruiting more times than I can count because I didn't want to go through another interview with another person that was not going to work out for my organization. Trust me, I feel your pain.

It is important to stick with it. Commit your time on the front end to help reduce the risk of a poor hire. Invest your time during the hiring process so you can benefit from a good hire for what you hope to be a long time. Skipping steps, making unbalanced decisions, and rushing through the process may result in a poor hiring choice. A poor hiring choice will cost you more time, money, and aggravation down the road; only to find out that you have to start over because you either had to terminate your bad hire or they quit. Either way, your position is open again and you are back at the beginning.

As I type this, I am sort of chuckling because you will rush and you will settle at some point in your professional career. In all likelihood, you will regret it. That said, we all do it. We all learn the hard way. You can read this over and over and you will still rush and settle at some point.

Some tips to help you commit the time:

1. Block out time in your schedule to interview. Leave the time blocked until you know for sure you don't need it. Once you start moving interview times around, you eventually give up all interview time for other things.

2. Do not double-book or over-book. If your day is too jammed, you will not be able to stay engaged in the interview. You will be worried about too many other things.

3. If you have a busy week, bump interviews to the next week. Yes, it is risky, but it will help you maintain your focus.

4. Do not allow any interruptions during interviews. Put your phone away, close your email and shut your door. Focus on the interview.

5. Don't schedule back-to-back interviews. It is exhausting.

6. Schedule interviews for the time of day when you know you are at your best. If you are a morning person, interview in the morning, etc.

7. Avoid lunch interviews. I am referring to interviewing while having a meal. It is too hard to focus, ask questions, stay on track and take notes all while you are trying to have a meal.

8. Interview in an office or conference room setting. Avoid restaurants or coffee shops. There are too many distractions.

9. If there are others in your office, let them know you are interviewing and that you should not be disturbed.

10. Finally, stay on schedule. If you constantly go over your time limit on your interviews, it will squeeze the rest of your day. Try to stay on track and finish your interviews within one hour, give or take.

Commit the time on the front end. Never settle.

CHAPTER SIX

FINALLY! Time to Start Interviewing

Now we are getting to the good stuff.

Your telephone screens are complete. You have narrowed your candidate pool down to two or three solid candidates. What's next? Full-on, face-to-face interviews.

It is always my personal preference to sit down, face-to-face, and interview candidates. I did not let the pandemic change this preference. We simply sat a little further apart. I like to see posture, body language, and eye contact. I like to learn about the energy of the candidate. I like to observe how candidates respond to questions and how they think through challenging questions. Oftentimes, these things are hard to determine on a video call. That said, if it is a remote position, it may be more time and cost effective to do a video interview. It is really your call. Either way, it's time to schedule some interviews.

Before scheduling interviews, determine if there is anyone else that will be involved in the interview process. It is important to let the candidate know, so they can be prepared for multiple interviews. It is also important to coordinate schedules.

Below are a few of my personal interviewing preferences for scheduling face-to-face interviews:
- Never schedule more than two face-to-face interviews in one day. If you interview all day, you get nothing else done and that will cause you stress.
- Try to get all face-to-face interviews within a few days of each other whenever possible.
- If you are interviewing for multiple positions, try not to schedule interviews for different roles on the same day. It just gets too confusing.

These tips will help you stay a little bit more organized during the interview process.

Create an email template to send to candidates with the following information for their face-to-face interview:
1. Address/Location of the interview
2. Location for parking
3. Any special instructions, eg: 3rd floor
4. How they should contact you upon arrival
5. Proper dress for the interview. Let your candidate know what is appropriate for your organization. It is always good to see how they do with it.
   I once had a candidate interview for a director level position. The candidate flew in from Florida. I was located in Ohio. The candidate came to the interview in a Hawaiian print shirt, shorts and boat shoes. Again, this was for a director level position. Spoiler alert, the candidate did not get the job.
6. Include the name and title of those that will be included in the interview process.
7. Give an approximate length of time for the interview.
8. The candidate will have your email address but include a telephone number in the event they need to reach you in transit.

Save this form for the future. With some luck and hard work, your business will continue to grow and you will need to hire more people.

A Candidate Interview Information Template is included in your Interview Deck in the back of the book.

There are online scheduling tools that are certainly an option for scheduling your interviews. It can be more complicated if there are multiple interviewers. I prefer to do my own scheduling so I can maintain control of my schedule/calendar.

If you are interviewing for more than one position, it is a good idea to try to schedule interviews grouped by position. Schedule for one position at the beginning of the week and the other at the end or if time allows, schedule a role per week.

The interviews are scheduled. Now it's time to move on to the interview questions.

CHAPTER SEVEN

Candidate Questions

If you don't have questions, how can you interview?

From a legal perspective, it's important to understand the questions you can and cannot ask your candidates. However, the *types* of questions you ask are also important. You are searching for someone great to be on your team.

This is an interview, be prepared for it. Don't try to wing it. An interview is *not* simply a conversation. This is your chance to understand your candidates and how they may or may not fit in your organization.

As I mentioned earlier, you will hit it off with some candidates, and you may not click with others. Whether or not you hit it off with a candidate has nothing to do with their ability to do the job. Reminder: **Hire the person that is the best overall fit for your organization.**

Let's talk about the types of questions to ask in an interview.

First, let's start with the questions you cannot ask. There are laws in place that protect candidates as well as employers. These laws are in place to ensure that employers make their hiring decisions based on the candidates' knowledge, skills, abilities, and fit within an organization. Your hiring decisions should be based on these things and these things alone.

Legal protection begins with Title VII of the Civil Rights Act of 1964. Title VII prohibits employment discrimination based on race, color, religion, sex, and national origin. It is critical that you are familiar with Title VII and have a full understanding of what you can and cannot discuss with your candidates.

Please understand that legal protections begin with Title VII, but those protections do not end at Title VII. All of the following are important to understand when considering candidates:

Title VII of the Civil Rights Act of 1964
The Americans with Disabilities Act
Americans with Disabilities Amendments Act
Equal Pay Act
Pregnancy Discrimination Act
Age Discrimination in Employment Act
Genetic Information Nondiscrimination Act (GINA)

See Additional Resources at the end of the book for more information.

Consideration of Title VII and all of these other Federal protection laws begins at the job posting, position description, and resume/CV review. They must continue throughout your hiring and employment process.

Federal employment protection law compliance applies to employers with 15 or more employees. Many of you reading this are small businesses and may not be fully impacted at this time. However, laws change and your business may grow. I suggest you begin to understand these employment laws now. Additionally, your state may have specific employment laws. Please make sure you are familiar with all applicable employment laws at federal, state and local levels.

I will simply say this: Do the right thing. Assess resumes/CVs, candidates, and interviews based on your business needs and candidate knowledge, skills, and abilities.

That said, as you are creating your list of questions, steer clear of anything in violation of Title VII, The ADA, and any other Federally protected class. If you need more information, please contact an employment attorney or a human resources professional. Don't be THAT employer.

Okay, let's move on to what you CAN ask your candidates.

An Interview Question Template is included in your Interview Deck in the back of the book. The template includes sample behavioral-based and cultural fit questions. It is important for you to include applicable technical questions. I have left you some space to include your technical fit questions.

The interview process is your chance to get to know your candidates and for them to get to know you. The intent of an interview question is not whether or not your candidate gets the right answer, in fact, in many cases, there is no right or wrong answer. The intent is to see how your candidate responds, how they draw on their own life and experiences to answer the questions. Create a list of thought-provoking questions.

- Does your candidate have the ability to think through the question?
- Can they respond appropriately within a reasonable amount of time?

The level of the position can help guide you to the level of depth to include in your list of questions. When creating your questions, I encourage three types of questions:

- Technical questions
- Behavior-based questions
- Cultural fit questions

Each type of question will help you gain insight into your candidate and determine what will work best for you, your open position, and your organization. You do not need too many of each, maybe 3 or 4 questions from each category. Finally, Avoid asking questions that will result in yes/no responses. However, if you do ask a question that results in yes or no, ask your candidate to elaborate.

For example: "*Do you have any spreadsheet work experience? If so, can you please tell me about it?*" If the phrase: "tell me about it" is excluded, you will receive a yes or a no response leaving much open to interpretation.

Keep your business goal in mind: **Hire the person that is the best overall fit for your organization.**

Behavioral-based questions

Behavioral-based questions are intended to dig into past experiences and how your candidate may have handled a situation. You can discuss how your candidate made their decisions and the outcome of those decisions. It seems obvious that someone early in their career may have fewer experiences but responses can be life-related as well as work-related.

Some examples of behavioral-based questions:
1. Tell me about a time when you made a mistake. What was the mistake, how did you handle it and what was the outcome?
2. Tell me about a time when you disagreed with a coworker. How did you work through the disagreement?

Cultural fit questions

Cultural fit questions are designed to understand if your candidate has the same values and behaviors that best fit within your organization. You want to build your organization with people that believe in you, your company and its mission. You want your business to be made up of people that want to help drive your success. To do that, they must believe in you, your mission, and how you run your business.

Some examples of cultural fit questions:
1. How do you like to be led?
2. Do you prefer to work independently or on a team? Why?

Technical fit questions

Technical fit questions or functional fit questions are the questions you create that apply to your open position. Ask questions related to the skill set needed to succeed in the role. These will vary significantly based on position. Once you have created them, save them. You may need them again someday. You can refer to your job description and job posting to build your technical fit questions.

As I mentioned earlier, I have provided a list of sample behavioral-based and cultural fit questions in your interview deck. If you don't like the questions I have provided, do an internet search. There are many options. The objective is not about using what has worked for me but rather to ask thought-provoking questions that work for you.

As you are interviewing your candidates, it is important to ask your entire candidate pool the same set of questions. By doing so, you will be better able to assess your candidates on a level playing field. You want to be able to compare apples to apples. Sure, there will be times when the conversation goes off the rails. That is perfectly fine. Go with it, but not for too long.

Do your best to stick to the script. If you get too far off course or take too much time on one question, you may not get through your list of questions in your allotted amount of time. Missing a question here or there is minor but you don't want to miss out on getting to know your candidate. Goal reminder: **Hire the person that is the best overall fit for your organization.** Never lose sight of the goal.

Interview Question Recap:
1. Try not to ask yes/no questions. If so, ask for elaboration.
2. Do not ask questions around protected class and privacy.
3. Ask technical questions that are relevant to the open position.
4. Ask thought-provoking questions.
5. Ask your candidate pool the same set of questions.
6. Stay on track.

Interviews are more than a simple conversation. You have to understand what your candidates can bring to the position and your company. When you interview, take the time and interview. Don't have an unplanned chit-chat. It does not provide insight into your candidates' knowledge, skills and abilities.

CHAPTER EIGHT

Beware of Interview Bias

Don't let your head get in the way of doing what is right.

What is interview bias? Interview bias is basing your hiring decision on factors that are not relevant for a candidate to succeed in the job. Interview bias can cause you to decide on a candidate, whether consciously or not, that is outside of the parameters of the "fit" for your open position.

There are many types of interview bias, and it is important to be aware of them. When you are considering your candidates, make sure you are considering them based on their technical and cultural fit within your organization.

Listed below are the different types of interview bias and brief descriptions.

1. **Central tendency bias** – this type of bias comes into play when using a rating system (of which I am not a fan). The interviewers tend to rate all candidates in the middle giving little to no differentiation between candidates. I don't like using a rating system so I have not experienced this bias. However, I have worked with business leaders that conduct performance evaluations with the same methodology. Not everyone is the same. Don't rate them as such.

2. **Contrast effect bias** – this type of bias occurs when a candidate may be compared to a prior candidate that was weaker or stronger. It may have you putting one candidate up against another candidate or employee. Don't do this. Assess all candidates based on skill set, fit and business need. Do not compare them to each other. Compare them with what is needed to succeed in the role.

3. **Cultural noise bias** – This type of bias can occur when a candidate answers questions in a way they think you want to hear -- the culturally acceptable response as opposed to their personal opinion. The bias can occur if you do not dig deep enough. If you ask a candidate whether or not they prefer to work alone or be part of a larger team, in nearly all cases, the candidate will respond that they can work in either situation. But...what if they actually loathe working on a team and just want to sit at their computer and do their work? Dig deep. For the record, I don't ask this question either. Your candidate will say they can do either because they want the job. Because you will typically get a response of "either", the question becomes irrelevant, providing no differentiation between candidates.

4. **First impression bias** – This bias occurs when you allow your first impressions or your first few interactions with the candidate to influence your hiring decision. I have been guilty of this one. I was interviewing for an administrative role. I had several interactions via email and telephone calls with a candidate, whom I will call Susan. I just loved Susan. We hit it off. We had several great conversations. When I sat down to interview Susan, I did not do a proper interview but rather talked about my vision for the future. I made the hire. I was only a few weeks into employment with Susan and I knew I made a mistake. It was my mistake. It was my fault and I knew it. I had to deal with my poor hiring decision. I ruined a relationship with someone I liked and yep, you guessed it, had to start back at the beginning. I didn't follow my own process. Don't make my mistake.

5. **Generalization bias** – generalization bias occurs when you assume a candidate's one-time action or behavior is always their behavior. I am not a fan of this bias description. Isn't action or behavior insight into a person's character? I would ask about the behavior in question, assuming it is not protected by Title VII. At the same time, are you going to make your decision based on a one-time mistake? Perhaps your candidate learned a valuable lesson. I will repeat, make your decision based on the person that most fits your role.

6. **Variable question bias** – Variable question bias occurs when you do not ask all candidates the same questions. I talk about this in Chapter seven. If you do not ask all candidates the same questions, how can you expect to equally assess them? Pulling from my example from #4, I did not ask this candidate the same questions as others because we hit it off. I made my decision based on the fact that we hit it off. Bad move.

7. **Negative emphasis bias** – This bias occurs if the candidate gives you a small amount of negative information and you allow that small amount of negative information to influence your hiring decision. If you have an interview that is all negative, that is an insight into someone who has the potential to be a negative person but perhaps not. Dig deep.

8. **Nonverbal bias** – Nonverbal bias occurs when you allow body language, eye contact, posture, or other nonverbal behaviors to negatively influence your hiring decision. A great example here is the difference between a salesperson versus an engineer. In my

experience, interviewing for these two roles draws a very different candidate pool. Decisions should be based on skill set, fit and business need. Can the candidate do the job?

9. **Recency bias** – Recency bias is when you base your hiring decision on the most recent candidate, most likely because you remember them best. In chapter Nine, I discuss the importance of taking good notes. This should help you avoid recency bias. Additionally, the chance of recency bias can be reduced by conducting all interviews within a few days, rather than spread out over a week or two.

These are a good sample of potential interview bias'. Consider where you may have interview bias or experienced interview bias. Be aware of interview bias and do not let bias influence your hiring decisions.

CHAPTER NINE

You Are in This Too!

How to stay engaged in the interview.

This is a great place for a goal reminder: **Hire the person that is the best overall fit for your organization.** You are invested in your business, why would you not be just as invested in the people you bring on board?

If you attempt to make a mad-dash through the interview and hiring process, you run some pretty big risks. The first of which is a poor hiring decision. I know, I know. There are no guarantees even if you take your time through the process. However, by committing time to the process, you will reduce some of the risks.

Sure, you can hire your sales manager's niece. After all, she needs a job; but is she the best person for the job? Will she care just because her uncle cares? On the front-end, it seems easier and quicker.

Maybe you will get lucky and she will be great. What are the odds? My recommendation is that if she really wants it, she can apply and go through the process with all the other candidates. No special treatment. No guarantees.

Promote your company

During your interviews, you have the opportunity to promote your business to your candidates. You can explain what you do and why you do it. You can help them understand what type of place you have created and why it is a great place to work. You are the face of the business and you are their first impression. Be ready. Be on. Be honest.

Because you are the candidate's first impression, you want to make sure you stay engaged during the interview. Pay attention to the conversation. For the love of everything good, put your phone away! If you are distracted or disengaged, your candidate will notice and may lose interest. Do your part. If you don't care, why should your candidate care?

Take good notes!
Taking good notes is critical to your process. You think you will remember who said what. You will not. I promise, you will not remember. In the Interview Deck at the back of this book, there is plenty of space to take notes. If you choose to use your own method, that is certainly your call, but please, take good notes. Good notes will also aid in your decision process. It will allow for a more level comparison of your candidates.

You can take notes during the interview or immediately following the interview. If you choose to take notes during the interview, let your candidate know that you are simply taking notes to keep your candidate interviews organized. You do not want them to wonder what you are doing or think you are distracted by something else.

If you choose to take notes after the interview, make sure you do it immediately following the interview. If you wait, you will forget. Yes, you will. I have interviewed many candidates over the years and tested both methods. I prefer to take notes immediately following an interview. For me, it was easier to stay engaged in the interview if I didn't have to write things down during the conversation. Do what works best for you.

You need to be careful with what you put in your notes. I learned this the hard way following legal action by a former employee. Don't learn the hard way. In your notes, write down only the candidate's responses to your questions. Stick to the facts of their response. If you feel this candidate is not going to be a good fit for your organization, it is fine to make note of why. It is not fine to write something that might be viewed as discriminatory against the candidate.

Here is the big note-taking mistake I made.

Much of my past HR life was in the manufacturing environment. I hired more engineers and project managers than I can count. I interviewed and hired many female project managers and engineers. However, in one case, during the interview, a female candidate told me that she was used to competing in a "man's world" and in fact, she saw it as a challenge. In my interview notes, I had written down the words, "man's world." I did not put any context behind those words.

Years later, that employee was terminated for performance. It seemed like a clean termination as we had well-documented performance issues and followed the right procedures. We had conversations about what needed to improve. When things didn't improve, we put the employee on a performance improvement plan. As things continued to get worse, we ultimately had to terminate the employee.

The employee filed a complaint with the EEOC. The words "man's world" in my interview notes were taken as discriminatory and those words worked against us – despite the fact that we had loads of documentation supporting poor performance.

The moral of this story is to use caution in your note-taking. Be clear on context. Be clear on what was said, why it was said, and who said it.

Let me give you another example...

You have two female candidates. They have similar backgrounds and on paper, both candidates meet the initial business need. You decide to interview both candidates.

Female Candidate #1: Throughout the interview, you discover the experience is similar to what you are trying to hire but not exactly what you want. This candidate is lacking a critical piece of experience. Additionally, despite your best efforts, you have a difficult time connecting with this candidate. Candidate #1 is pregnant.

Female Candidate #2: Candidate #2 brings more relevant experience as well as an immediate connection to you and what you do.

In your notes for candidate #1, you document where her experience is disconnected from your business needs. You also jot down the word "pregnant" in a corner on one of your sheets of notes.

In your notes for candidate #2, you document how her experience is a match for your business needs. You also document how the conversation seemed more natural and how her responses seemed more appropriate for your business and its vision.

You make candidate #2 a job offer. Candidate #1 thinks she did not get the offer because she was pregnant. While that is not the reason she did not get the offer, the fact that you wrote down the word pregnant in your notes raises a potential red flag. It could be perceived that you did not hire her because she was pregnant.

Pregnancy is protected under the ADA, and you will likely face legal action if candidate #1 decides she was discriminated against and chooses to pursue action. The word pregnant is completely irrelevant to the skill set and qualification for this role. What was the value in writing it down? If you don't need it, don't write it.

Use caution in your note-taking. Take good, clear, definitive, fact-based notes.

Body language
You can learn so much by observing your candidates' body language. Some behaviors are obvious, some are more subtle. All can be telling. Reading body language is a skill that you develop over time. There are some basics you can keep on your radar.
1. Is your candidate comfortable?
2. Do they struggle to find words? Are they responsive to your questions?
3. How do their responses and actions relate to your business needs?
4. How is their posture? Are they sitting professionally or slouching in the chair?
5. How is their eye contact? Are they gazing around the room?

Any or all of these things can be good, bad, right, or wrong, depending on the role you are filling.

For example, if you are hiring a salesperson, you likely want someone dynamic. You want them to have some energy with the ability to provide an articulate, clear response to your questions. If you are hiring an engineer, you may not care about their less-than-out-going-behavior as long as they show they have the technical depth you desire for your business.

While keeping your business goal at the forefront of your interview, keep an eye on the subtle behaviors and what will make the best fit for your role.

The awkward silence
When interviewing candidates, there is often an awkward silence. Candidates are considering their answer, perhaps trying to figure out either how to answer or how to answer the way they think you want them to answer.

Regardless of why, allow for that silence. Do not prompt or prod your candidate. See how they handle it. Allow them to search for their words and their response. You can learn from this situation. The interviewer will often feel a need to fill the space with words. DON'T! Let the silence play out. Yep, it is awkward. So what? Let your candidate resolve it.

Candidate consideration
As you are considering your candidates, it seems like a good time to remind you of the goal: ***Hire the person that is the best overall fit for your organization.***

In my experience, there are usually one or two candidates that rise above all others. It is a good problem to have to choose between a couple of qualified candidates. A difficult choice is far better than the alternative, which is not feeling great about any of your candidates. It is great if there is one candidate that sets themselves apart from others. Your decision is easily made.

How do you choose between two candidates? Based on your job description and the flow and ease of the conversation, which candidate checks the most skill set and business need boxes? In addition to your technical and organizational fit outcomes, you may also want to consider your candidate's motivation and their willingness to learn and grow within your organization.

It is highly unlikely that your candidates are in a dead heat but if they are, go with your gut. Again, it is a good problem to have to choose between two qualified candidates.

This is a decision that will make an impact on your business in the future. Take your time. Review the candidates carefully. Choose. Never settle.

This new hire is an investment. Do your best to do it right. Commit to this process. Yes, it is hard. It is risky. It is time-consuming. Yes to all of those things. At the same time, consider the alternatives...poor hires cost time and money.

CHAPTER TEN

Commit the Time
Never Settle
Final Round

Seriously? Again?

I have discussed "commit the time" throughout this book. I am sure you have picked up by now that I am trying to drive the point home. I cannot stress this enough. This is not a process you want to rush.

Business leaders would constantly tell me, "this position is a rush, get it filled as quickly as possible." Ok, first, why would I not work towards filling it as quickly as possible? That was always a bit insulting, as though I did not understand the urgency. I would tell them I could fill any role they need by next week, but I could not make any promises about the quality of the candidate. Interviewing and reviewing candidates is a time investment. It is an investment in your business. You cannot rush the process and you cannot settle. The powers that be usually got the message. For the record, in nearly every case of rushing and settling, we experienced regret. Imagine that!

The next major point that I cannot say loud enough, often enough, or emphasize enough is **NEVER SETTLE**. Never settle on a candidate. If you are saying to yourself, that candidate is *good enough*, you should not hire them. You have to feel certain about your new hire. You have to see potential in your new hire. If you are settling, you will likely feel the pain in the future.

Yes. I have done it. I have settled on a candidate, and it backfired every time. I had to learn the hard way. Never settle. If you are not feeling the strength you need in your candidates (and I know this sounds grueling) – start over. I can feel you shaking your head at me. The thought of starting this process all over, of taking the time to review, screen, interview. Ugh! Trust me, you will be happier in the long run if you take the time to find the right candidate for your role and for your business.

As I was writing this, I decided to contact some of my awesome former colleagues to talk about times they **settled** on a candidate/hire. Yes, they have done it, too. I contacted several leaders that I worked with and hired for while I was in my HR role. I asked them whether or not the hire worked out.

It was unanimous. Never settle. The list of those that worked out was far smaller than the list of regrets. When they provided me with examples, nine out of ten did not work out. On a rare occasion, you get lucky and one works out.

They sighted example after example of times they settled. In nearly every case, not only did they have to ultimately terminate the poor hiring decision, and start the entire process from the beginning but, it also cost the company time, money, and workforce setbacks. No good comes from settling on your hiring decision.

You have to get rid of your fear of saying no to your candidates and/or your peers. You cannot offer everyone a job. You have one open position. You have an expectation of how this position should impact your business. Why would you settle? What is the value of settling?

Hold out for the best candidate. It will pay off. Have the courage to say no. If it doesn't feel right, chances are, it isn't right. Trust your gut. Don't do it.

Here is an example of a time when a Chief Human Resource Officer settled on a high-level candidate and it ended badly. The position was to lead division operations. This role was the highest achievable role at the division level.

The head of HR for the entire organization was against the hire. He voiced his opinion, but at the time did not put up a big enough argument as the rest of the interview team agreed. This person, we'll call him John, was hired for the role, and within 6 months, he was terminated. His "management" style was against the very core values of our organization. He damaged employee morale and good employees resigned during his brief tenure.

The entire search had to begin...again. Damage to employee morale not only caused issues in the day-to-day of the office and manufacturing plant but also gave employees a reason to question the trust of the executive leadership team. The damage took months, even years to repair. The financial burden to the organization was staggering. Who needs that?

Don't be afraid to keep searching. The market is ever-changing and there are new candidates available daily. Timing matters when it comes to the hiring process. Sometimes you have to be patient and wait for the right candidate to find you or for you to find them.

Do not get discouraged. If there is one thing we can count on, it is change. This is true in life, at work, and with the candidate search process.

During my tenure at my prior company, we were interviewing for a Manager of Operations in the manufacturing facility. We were exhausted by countless interviews over several months. We just couldn't find the right person for the job.

Late to the game was a dynamic candidate that seemed to check all of the boxes. We conducted multiple interviews that included several business leaders. The candidate said everything right.

At the end of the interview process, the hiring manager decided to move forward with an offer. The hiring manager said to me, "He is either going to be great at this job or he is full of shit." The hiring manager was concerned that we were settling. Sadly, the candidate was full of it and we had to replace him.

The point is sometimes the candidate can sell themselves better than we can detect. No one is a perfect interviewer.

Commit the time. Never settle.

CHAPTER ELEVEN

Make the Offer

Why it's important to be ready with your offer.

You put in the time, and I know you don't want to do it again, so don't allow some other company to snag your best candidate. Once you have made your decision on a candidate, move quickly. Your candidates are actively looking for work. They are ready to make a move. Don't make them wait. Be prepared with an offer, and make it. If you don't, someone else might, and guess where that leaves you...back at the beginning.

Call your candidate and give them the verbal offer. Let them know a written offer is coming, and go over some of the highlights. Get them excited about the opportunity. Let your candidate know their offer will be in their inbox within 24 hours. It does not take days or even a week to create an offer, especially if you have done your homework upfront. Be ready, keeping in mind that everything you do during this phase is part of your pitch to get your new hire. If candidates have a bad experience during the offer process, it reflects on you and your organization.

I think you get the point. If you have a candidate that you want to hire, don't wait. Make the offer! Make your move.

Please, do not forget to follow up with those you did not choose. It is a matter of respect and a reflection on your business. There is no nice way to do it, but there is a respectful way to do it. I have provided you with a template, but it is just that, a template. Please personalize the rejection letter. It will help soften the blow and shows that you operate with integrity. You may cross paths again. Do the right thing.

An Offer Letter Template and a Rejection Letter Template are included in your Interview Deck in the back of the book.

CHAPTER TWELVE

Just a Few More Things...

You're almost ready!

Organize your process

Do your best to organize your process and keep it organized. It is easy to let things go as your real job gets in the way. Keep resumes, interview notes, and other related documents together. If you are interviewing for more than one position, this step becomes more critical. Using the interview deck included in this book will help, especially as you are getting started.

It doesn't matter if you use electronic or paper interview decks. Do what works best for you. It is the organization of your open positions, candidates, and notes that is important, not the method you choose.

Using an interview template will simplify your ability to be consistent. It will also provide you with a framework for your interviews and keep you organized. Please, if you are not comfortable with what I have provided, I encourage you to create your own template.

What happens when your process is not organized? One of the biggest mistakes in my career occurred when I was disorganized and rushed to extend an offer. I extended the offer, but to the wrong candidate. NOT COOL!!! It is a horrible feeling to make a telephone call to a candidate and explain my huge mistake. Don't do what I did. Get organized and don't be in such a hurry that you make mistakes.

Fear

Fear can be a heavy barrier. Don't let it get in your way. Do not allow fear to keep you from advancing your business. Your business needs change and hiring will help you grow and change. The biggest fear with regard to hiring is making a poor hiring decision. If you do make a poor hire, deal with it head on.

Dealing with a poor hiring decision
The most critical part of dealing with a poor hiring decision is just that – dealing with it. Poor hiring decisions happen. That is just how things go sometimes. The most harm that a poor hiring decision can bring to your business is if you do not deal with the poor hire. A poor organizational fit can damage morale, trust and in some cases damage business processes. Deal with the problem and deal with it quickly.

You must first assess the problem. Does your candidate have the ability to do the role for which they were hired? If you are convinced they do, then figure out why they are not performing as expected. Are you providing direction? Do they understand your expectations? Have you clearly defined their tasks? If not, I suggest you do so. You cannot expect performance from someone that does not know or understand what to do.

If you are providing them with all of the tools they need to be successful? Do they have proper training? Proper hardware and software? If not, get it for them. If they have proper tools and training, look a little deeper.

If you determine that you have provided tools, training, priorities, and goals, then it may be a poor fit within your organization. To find out, first, start with a conversation. Do not be afraid of the conversation. Remember your goal when you set out to fill this position: ***Hire the person that is the best overall fit for your organization.***

Talk to your new hire. Find out what is going on with them. Ask what they need to succeed. Clearly state your expectations. Clearly state what they are doing well and what needs to happen for this relationship to work out. Make it clear that failure to improve may lead to further action. They must understand your expectations.

- Start with a conversation
- Set goals and expectations
- Discuss milestones to achieve these improvements
- Confirm dates
- Follow-up
- *Hold them and yourself accountable*

If things do not improve, I would advise a separation. Yes, separations are difficult, but they are necessary when all else fails. If they are done properly, with dignity, respect, and open communication, they can be less painful. Don't get me wrong, they suck, but being prepared for the conversation eases the stress. Do the right thing and do it the right way.

Move forward. Always continue to move forward.

CHAPTER THIRTEEN

Wrap-Up

We are almost done.
I mean it this time.

Interviewing is a skill that is honed over time. The more you do it, the better you get. You learn to become aware of the little things. You learn what types of people, personalities, and skill sets find the most success within your organization.

The toughest part of this process is having the patience to do it properly and dealing with frustration if you cannot find the right person for your role. The best advice I can give is:

- Do your best to be patient.
- Recognize that an instant connection does not mean it is the most qualified person for your business needs.
- Don't lose sight of your ultimate goal: **Hire the person that is the best overall fit for your organization.**
- Commit the time.
- Never settle.

There are times it can be painful and there are times when you simply get exhausted by the process. Push through the discomfort and do not settle for less than what you want for your business.

A key takeaway from this book is not about doing things my way. It is about developing an organized process. Build a process that works for you. Do the prep work. Ask questions that work for you. Save everything!

It is about committing the time to the interview process, despite the pain. It is about finding the best candidate for your organization. Finally, it is about never settling on a candidate that is *good enough*.

Find great people. Build a great organization with great people. Do great things.

Additional Resources

Here is a list of important websites for reference during your interviewing and hiring process. This information is included on my website at HRCreativeConsulting.com/bookresources

Equal Employment Opportunity Commission
https://www.eeoc.gov/

A reference guide to The Fair Labor Standards Act
https://www.dol.gov/agencies/whd/compliance-assistance/handy-reference-guide-flsa

Title VII of the Civil Rights Act of 1964
https://www.eeoc.gov/statutes/title-vii-civil-rights-act-1964

The Americans with Disabilities Act and Americans with Disabilities Amendments Act: ADA.gov
https://www.ada.gov/

The Pregnancy Discrimination Act of 1978 | U.S. Equal Employment Opportunity Commission
https://www.eeoc.gov/statutes/pregnancy-discrimination-act-1978

The Equal Pay Act of 1963
https://www.eeoc.gov/statutes/equal-pay-act-1963

The Age Discrimination in Employment Act of 1967
https://www.eeoc.gov/statutes/age-discrimination-employment-act-1967

The Genetic Information Nondiscrimination Act of 2008 | U.S. Equal Employment Opportunity Commission
https://www.eeoc.gov/statutes/genetic-information-nondiscrimination-act-2008

This list will get you started, but it is not an all-inclusive list. It is important to be familiar with employment law at the federal, state and local level.

INTERVIEW DECK

Interview Checklist

- [ ] Understand the business need
- [ ] Determine tasks to be completed
- [ ] Complete position assessment
- [ ] Determine method for sourcing candidates
- [ ] Post position. Begin sourcing candidates
- [ ] Resume review. Identify top 6-8 best candiates
- [ ] Telephone screen top candidates
- [ ] Schedule interviews for top 3 candidates
- [ ] Prepare for interviews by creating interview folders for each candidate
- [ ] Become familiar with employment law
- [ ] Select top candiate
- [ ] Make the offer

Commit the time. Never settle.

Position Assessment

Position _____

Salary or Hourly _____ (Determined by the FLSA)

Full-time or Part-time _____

Salary Range _____

Office - Remote - Hybrid _____

Hiring manager _____

Education requirements _____

Experience level _____

Position task list:

This list should include the must-haves for success in this role

_____
_____
_____
_____
_____
_____
_____
_____
_____
_____
_____
_____
_____
_____
_____
_____
_____
_____
_____
_____
_____
_____
_____
_____
_____
_____
_____
_____
_____
_____
_____

Candidate Telephone Screen

Candidate name: _____ **Date of telephone screen:** _____

Position: _____ **Schedule Interview** (Date) _____

Salary range: _____ **Decline candidate** _____

Telephone screen Questions:

Can you tell me why you are looking for a new opportunity?

_____
_____
_____

Can you tell me why you are interested in this opportunity?

_____
_____
_____

The salary range for this position is ($X - $X (have your salary ranges prepared))
Does this range meet your expectations?

*In many states, it is illegal to ask candidates their current salary but it is important to understand expectations.

_____
_____

Can you walk me through your resume?

_____
_____
_____
_____
_____
_____
_____
_____

Notes:

_____
_____
_____
_____
_____
_____
_____

Interview Information Email Template

Dear <Candidate's name>,

We look forward to meeting you on Interview date & time.

Our address is below, as well as my telephone number, if needed. Upon arrival, you <Provide parking and building entrance information>. From the lobby, dial my extension XXX and I will be up to meet you.

Our office attire is casual so please feel free to dress accordingly.

Again, we look forward to meeting you.
Sincerely,

Your name
Your number

Business address

**This is a generic form that you can customize for your business and save the document for future use.

Candidate Interview Questions

Position: _____   Interview Date: _____

Salary range: _____

Candidate Name: _____   Proceed with offer: ____ YES   ____ NO

Desired pay: _____

Date: _____

Interview team: _____

Cultural fit questions

Tell me a little bit about yourself
This is an icebreaker question to get the conversation going. Candidates can discuss professional or personal situations. I have had it go either way.

_____
_____
_____
_____

Tell me about the first job that you did for which you got paid. Tell me what you learned from that experience.

_____
_____
_____
_____

Other than your family, tell me what is most important to you.
If you do not exclude family, everyone will say family. It is the easy answer.

_____
_____
_____
_____

Describe your ideal leader.

_____
_____
_____
_____

What about this role/position is of interest to you?

_____
_____
_____
_____

How would your coworkers describe you?

_____
_____
_____
_____

Tell me about a mistake you made at work. How did you handle it?

_____
_____
_____
_____

What is your favorite thing about your current job? Least favorite?

_____
_____
_____
_____

HRCreativeConsulting.com   Copyright ©2023 by Kristin Heller

Candidate Interview Questions

Behavior-based questions

Tell me about a time when you had a conflict with a coworker. How did you handle it?

Tell me about a time when you failed at something. How did you handle it?

Tell me about a time when you feel you went above and beyond. Why did you do it? What was the outcome?

You are given a new assignment. It is the first of its kind. What do you do first?

What do you see as your greatest strength? Weakness?

Everything is due at the same time. Things are crazy busy. Dates are fast approaching. What do you do first? How do you prioritize your work?

Tell me about a time you disagreed with your boss. How did you handle it?

Tell me about the most difficult problem you have had to solve at work.

Candidate Interview Questions

Technical Questions: This section is for questions specific to the role.

Notes:

*Choose 3 or 4 questions from each section. It is not necessary to ask all the questions listed.
Find out what works best for you.

Make sure you are familiar with what you can and cannot ask in an interview. See below for information.

The Civil Rights Act of 1964 Title VII
www.eeoc.gov/statutes/title-vii-civil-rights-act-1964

Offer Letter Template

Candidate Name
Street Address
City, State Zip

Dear <Insert Candidate Name>
I am excited to extend you the following employment offer as a/an <Insert Position Title>. You will report directly to <Insert Manager Name>. Your start date will be <Insert Start Date>.

Your salary will be <$Insert Annual Salary> per year and will be paid <insert pay frequency>.

Include if applicable
Incentive Pay
You are eligible for an annual incentive of (XX%), which is paid at the sole discretion of Management, as aligned with <Insert company name> performance and business targets. The amount is dependent upon achievement of specific company performance targets during the fiscal year. This incentive also takes into account your personal performance based on specific goals set for you.

Define any incentive policies

PTO/Vacation:
Include vacation allowance here.

Benefits:
- ☐ Health Care
- ☐ 401k
- ☐ Life Insurance/AD&D
- ☐ Holidays
- ☐ Etc…

Include attachments defining additional benefits.

Sincerely

<Name>
<Title>
<Email address>

Offer Letter Template

Terms of offer:
If you do any pre-employment testing, ie: drug screening or background checks, it should be included in the terms of the offer. Additionally, you will want to include an expiration date of the offer stating it will be withdrawn, if not accepted by said date. Include any non-compete information at this time as well.

By signing/accepting this offer, you acknowledge that you have read, understood and accept this offer and agree to the terms and conditions of employment.

Acknowledged, Accepted and Agreed
<Candidate Signature>
<Candidate Print Name>
<Date>

REMINDERS:
- **Make the offer as soon as you have made your decision. Don't risk losing your first choice.**
- **It is important for you to include your company benefit information to provide your candidate with a full understanding of the total compensation.**
- **Always, always, always get the acceptance (including any negotiations) in writing or electronically via email. Do not consider a verbal acceptance as final.**

Thank you for your interest letter

Candidate Name
Street Address
City, State Zip

Dear <Insert Candidate Name>
Thank you for your interest in <Insert Company Name> and the position of <Insert Job Title>.
After careful review of applicants, unfortunately, at this time we are unable to invite you to the next stage of the hiring process. Though your resume was impressive, we have decided to move forward with a candidate whose qualifications are better suited to this particular role.

However, we hope you will apply again in the future if you see a job opening more suited to your qualifications.

We wish you success in your career.

Once again, thank you for your interest in our company.

Sincerely,
Name
Title
Email address

PDF versions of the Interview Deck
templates can be found at:

HRCreativeConsulting.com/BookResources

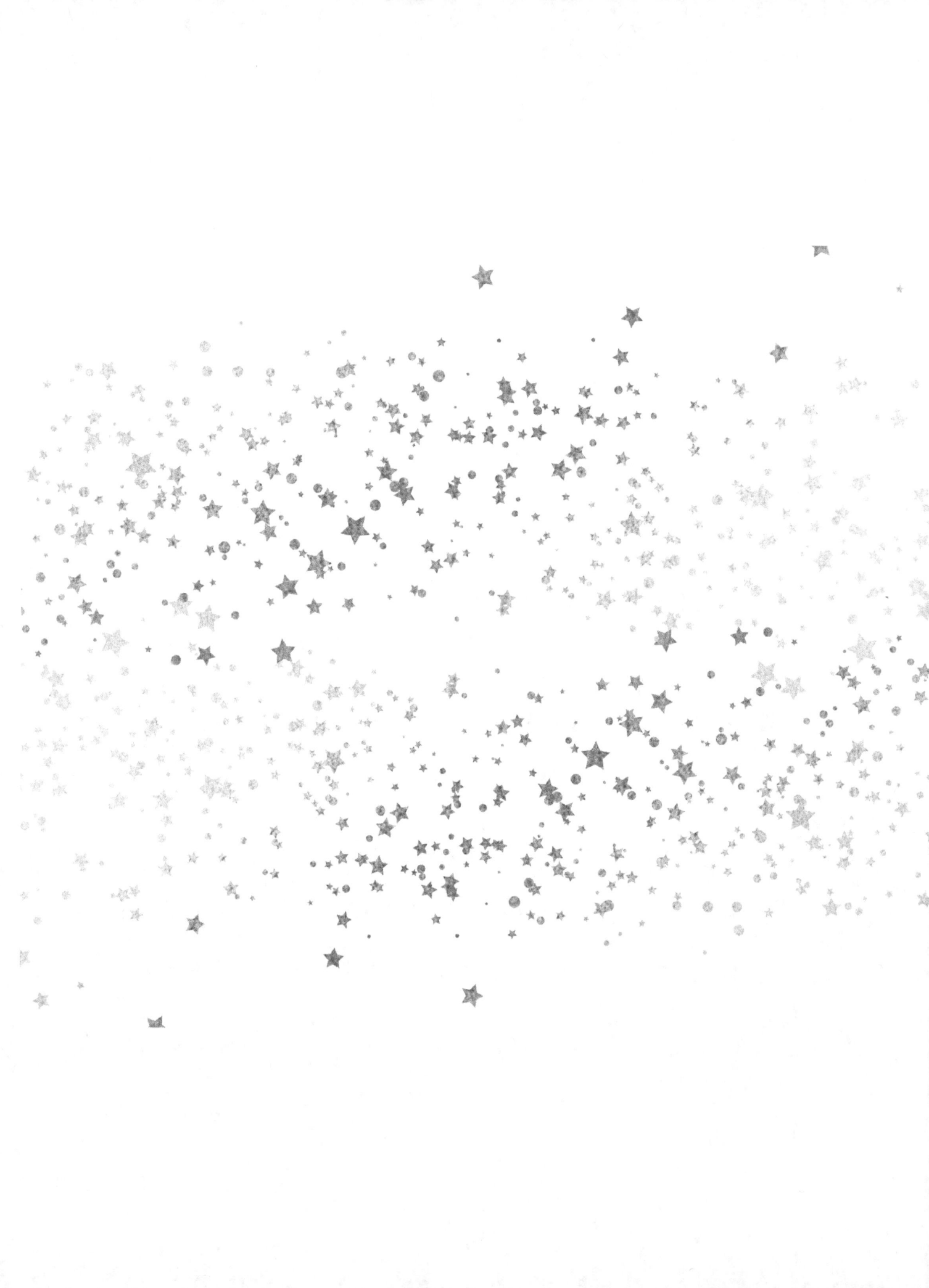

IT'S TIME TO MAKE
A GREAT HIRE

NO MORE
HIRING
REGRETS

www.ingramcontent.com/pod-product-compliance
Lightning Source LLC
Chambersburg PA
CBHW081101240526
45465CB00026B/3068